JAMES IV:
A RENAISSANCE KING

First published in Great Britain
in Merlins in 1996

HB ISBN 0 86241 639 6

PB ISBN 0 86241 655 8

Cataloguing-in-Publication Data
*A catalogue record for this title is
available upon request from the British
Library*

The publisher acknowledges subsidy from the Scottish Arts Council
towards publication of this volume

Typeset and designed by
Artisan Graphics, Edinburgh

Printed and bound by
Oriental Press, Dubai

CANONGATE BOOKS LTD
14 HIGH STREET EDINBURGH EH1 1TE

Many nobles resented the new parliament. They also resented the new King's failure to reward them. Some of them joined forces, taking James III's *bloody serk* (blood-stained shirt) as their banner. But the new King had defeated them by December 1489.

Establishing Control

Some of the nobles who opposed the new Parliament were based at Dumbarton Castle, towering over the Firth of Clyde on Dumbarton Rock. Royal armies laid siege to the castle, and the nobles inside were joined by other rebels dissatisfied with the King. These rebel forces drove off the besieging army and set out for Aberdeen to join forces with Lord Forbes, who had been loyal to King James III. They met the King's army near Aberfoyle, and were defeated.

A similar siege at Duchal Castle ended with the rebels surrendering when the King's army brough the great cannon Mons Meg from Edinburgh Castle.

James IV realised that the best way to prevent rebellions was to give the whole country a strong system of law and order. In those days, criminals were dealt with in local *justice ayres*, or open-air courts. There was no national police force to enforce the law. Justice ayres were held all over the country in the spring and autumn each year. James himself attended many ayres to see that his laws were kept.

There was no paper money in fifteenth century Scotland. The only coins were silver pennies, demys and lions.

However, it is almost impossible to compare the values of these coins with money today because most people used produce, such as grain, meat, eggs or firewood to exchange for anything they wanted to buy. They even used produce to pay their rents and taxes.

Wrongdoers at this time could be severely punished. In 1504, James spent some weeks supervising the hanging of criminals in Eskdale. He also organised a raid on Teviotdale, bringing prisoners to court at Jedburgh with nooses already round their necks. That incident was ironically called *Jeddart Justice.*

Punishment was not always as harsh as this. The king's presence was often enough to bring people to order. The ayres could also prove a useful source of money for the crown. A criminal might be given a *grant of remission*, which meant that he was allowed to pay a fine to make up for his crime, instead of being sent to prison. The fine was often very large — as much as £50 for one offence. After one justice ayre, Lord Drummond had gathered £1695 for the King. This was a vast sum of money for those days.

There were also civil courts which dealt with disputes between people who had not broken the law. James set up a *conciliar session*, made up of councillors and judges, to hear civil cases. This was an early version of our modern Court of Session, and James himself often acted as judge in these sessions.

James IV gradually strengthened his control over his government and people. He was willing to use force, but he could also be lenient when he thought this was the best course of action. But while Lowland Scotland began to obey the King's laws, his rule was less established amongst the Highland clans. James realised that he would have to pay special attention to the Highlanders.

Flodden

Why was the Battle of Flodden fought, and why were the Scots so decisively beaten? The most important thing to remember about the Battle of Flodden is that it was part of a European war. On one side were Spain, England, and the Papal States. On the other side were France and Scotland.

The Pope, Julius II, was ambitious. He was not only head of the Church, but he was also an important ruler. The Papal States were part of what we now call Italy, and Pope Julius wanted to enlarge his territories by driving the French out of Milan, which they occupied. But the Pope's army was defeated by the French, who then invaded the Papal States.

Julius asked Ferdinand, King of Spain, and the young Henry VIII, King of England, to join him in a 'Holy League' against the French. Henry was a strong ally. He had ships, money, and a good army — and he wanted an excuse to invade France, since he believed that part of France belonged to England. But he was worried that Scotland might invade England while he was away.

Europe in the reign of James IV

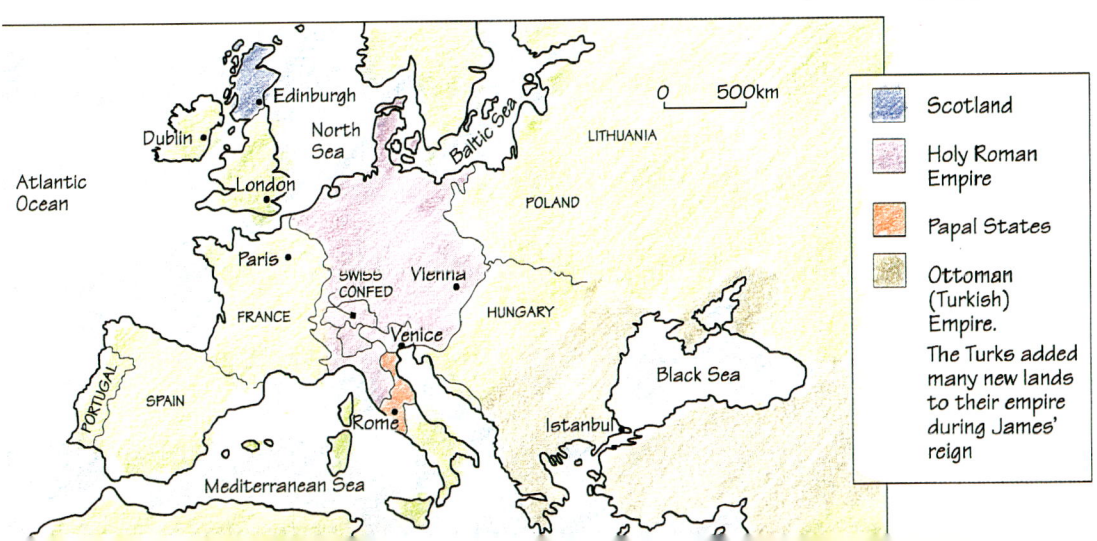

This situation worried King James. France was Scotland's ally, even though a Treaty of Perpetual Peace had been signed with England in 1502. If James did nothing while Henry invaded France, then perhaps Scotland would be Henry's next target. Henry VIII had also shown himself to be a less peaceful man than his father. He had broken the Perpetual Peace when his ships attacked *The Lion* and the *Jenny Pirwin*, and killed Andrew and Robert Barton. James did not trust Henry: he felt that he had to help the French by attacking England. But if he did this, it would mean that he had publicly broken the Treaty of Perpetual Peace he had signed with England.

King Henry VIII sailed to France with an invading army in 1513. He left a second army at home under the command of the Earl of Surrey. "My lord," he said to Surrey before he sailed, "I trust not the Scots, therefore I pray you be not negligent." On 11 August 1513, a Scottish herald arrived at Henry's camp in France with a letter from King James IV. The letter said that if Henry did not return to England at once, James and his army would invade. "Tell thy master," said Henry VIII, "that I have left an earl in my realm at home that shall be able to defeat him and all his power." England and Scotland were at war.

Throughout August the King's army assembled outside Edinburgh. Over twenty thousand men gathered from all parts of Scotland — lords in full armour with sword and pike, mounted on fine Flemish horses; yeomen dressed in steel jackets and helmets carrying pikes 5.5 metres long; Borderers wearing red tunics over their steel jackets, bearing swords and lances 2.5 metres long; and the Highlanders in their belted plaids, armed with their great claymores and light bows and arrows.

An English soldier carrying a halberd *or* bill.

The victorious English camp after the Battle of Flodden

After the Battle

Scotland now waited for an English invasion, but it never came. Winter approached, and the English army was tired and wanted to go home. James's corpse was taken to Berwick and then to London. There were rumours that the King was not dead and that he had been seen riding from the battlefield.

Scotland was now without a king. Many of the nation's young men were dead. More than forty lords had died at Flodden, and the country which had been united under King James IV would soon be divided again.

Six weeks after Flodden, there was a rebellion in the Highlands, and there was no strong king this time to keep the peace. James V was only two years old. As one writer said,

> "Men were in good hope, if the will of Almighty God had lent him [James IV] longer life, he would have brought the realm of Scotland to such flowering estate as was never yet heard of."

Acknowledgements

The publishers are grateful to the following organisations and individuals for permission to reproduce the illustrations.

The front cover shows a detail of a portrait of James IV by an unknown artist, reproduced by permission of the Scottish National Portrait Gallery. The background image is a section of James IV's court records, from the Scottish Record Office. *Page 5, 29* The Royal Collection, © Her Majesty The Queen: *pages 6, 33* Sir Francis Oglivy, Bart: *pages 7, 9, 11 bottom, 12, 14 bottom left. 15 bottom, 19, 39 centre* Historic Scotland: *pages 8, 11 top, 14 top, 16, 23 bottom, 32 bottom, 33 right, 34* National Museums of Scotland: *page 13* Scottish National Portrait Gallery: *pages 15 top, 21, 25, 26, 37 bottom, 38 bottom, 40* National Library of Scotland: *page 18* Castle Arms, Edinburgh: *pages 20, 22* Crown Copyright: Royal Commission on the Ancient and Historic Monuments of Scotland: *page 28 top* Edinburgh Public Libraries: *page 28 bottom, page 30 top* Scottish Record Office: *page 31 top, 36 top right, 36 bottom* Mansell Collection: *page 31 bottom* by courtesy of the National Portrait Gallery, London: *page 35* National Gallery of Scotland: *page 38 top* Glasgow University Library: *page 39 top and bottom left* National Trust for Scotland: *page 43* The Clann: *page 44* reproduced by kind permission of the Faculty of Advocates. Every effort has been made to trace holders of copyright, and we apologise to any whom it has proved imposible to contact.